KU-228-106

CONTENTS

WHO WERE THE VIKINGS?

The Vikings came from Norway, Denmark and Sweden. They attacked the coasts of northern Europe from around 800 to 1100 CE, bringing terror to peaceful places. They stole money, destroyed houses and churches, and captured people to sell as slaves. But the Vikings were not just bloodthirsty bandits. They were tough sailors, clever **merchants**, skilful craftworkers and bold explorers. They were also hard-working **settlers**, who built new farms, villages, forts and towns.

Small, silver head showing a Viking warrior, found in Aska, Sweden. No one knows who he was or where he fought and died.

The Viking homelands in northern Europe were surrounded by stormy seas to the east, west and south, and by Arctic ice to the north. ▶

ICELAND   NORWAY

GREENLAND

SWEDEN

ATLANTIC OCEAN

NEWFOUNDLAND

DENMARK   RUSSIA

Normandy

DID YOU KNOW?

THESE ARE ALL VIKING WORDS: BOTH, DRAG, EGG, FALL, GALE, KNIFE, SCORE, SCOLD, SHIP, SLING, SLUG, SMILE, WANT, WHIRL, WHISTLE, WINDOW AND WING.

JARLS AND THINGS

The first Viking lands were ruled by **jarls** (nobles). Over time, as Viking society grew larger, the most successful jarls became kings. Viking villagers held public meetings, called 'Things', once a year to decide how their communities should be run.

Monster face with horns and a long beard carved on a stone in Viking Denmark. ▶

VIKING WANDERERS

Viking kings, jarls and ordinary people travelled vast distances to trade and find new land. Wherever they settled, they brought their own language, beliefs, traditions and skills. Even today, many places in Europe have Viking names, and north European languages contain Viking words.

4

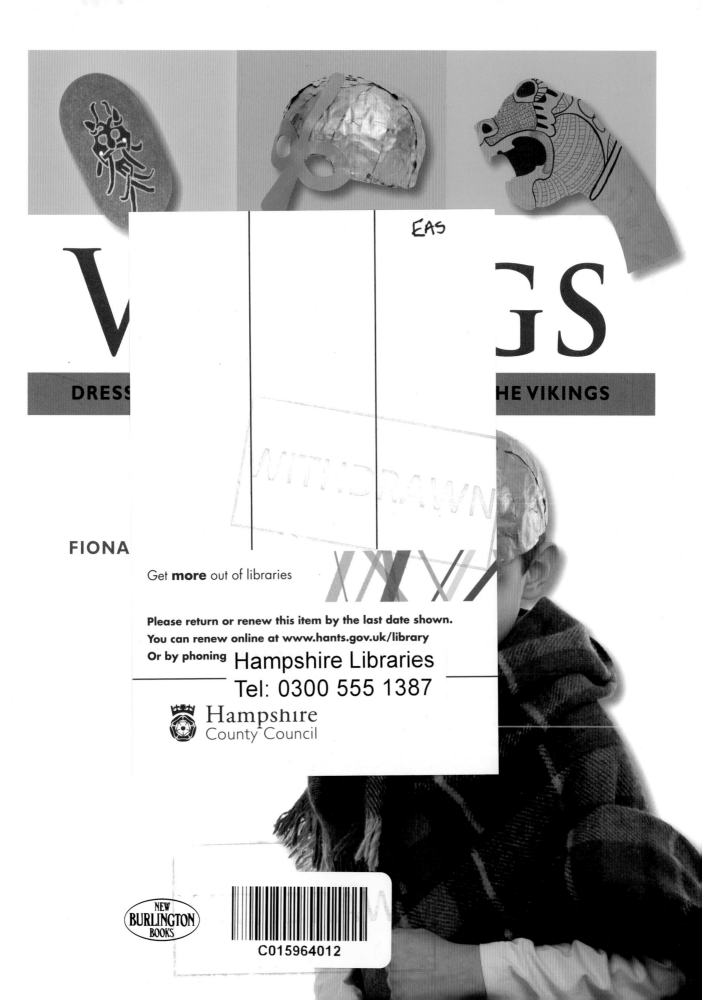

V GS

DRESS ... HE VIKINGS

FIONA

EAS

NEW
BURLINGTON
BOOKS

A NEW BURLINGTON BOOK
The Old Brewery
6 Blundell Street
London N7 9BH

Copyright © QED Publishing 2007

First published in the UK in 2007 by
QED Publishing
A Quarto Group company
226 City Road
London EC1V 2TT

www.qed-publishing.co.uk

A catalogue record for this book is available from the
British Library.

ISBN 978 1 78171 493 5

Written by Fiona Macdonald
Editor Felicity Fitchard
Designer Liz Wiffen
Projects made by Veronica Erard

Publisher Steve Evans
Creative Director Zeta Davies
Senior Editor Hannah Ray

Printed and bound in China

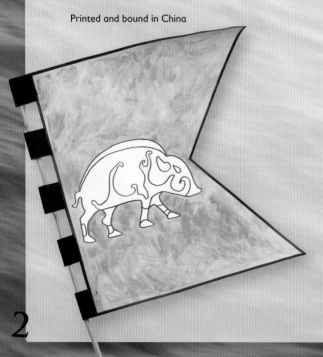

Picture credits

Key: t = top, b = bottom, c = centre, l = left, r = right,
fc = front cover

akg-images: p6 tr Jürgen Sorges.

The Art Archive: p4 br Prehistoric Museum Moesgard
Høberg Denmark/Dagli Orti; p8 tl, p20 tl Musée de la
Tapisserie Bayeux/Dagli Orti.

Corbis: p28 tl: Charles & Josette Lenars.

Dorling Kindersley: p12 tr; p14 tr Alan Keohane; p18
bl Geoff Dann; p28 cb Peter Anderson/Danish National
Museum.

TopFoto: p26 tr.

Werner Forman Archive: FC, p16 tl Universitetets
Oldsaksamling, Oslo; p4 tl, p8 br, p14 bl Statens
Historiska Museum, Stockholm; p6 bl National Museum,
Denmark; p10 tl Bergen Maritime Museum; p10 bl Viking
Ship Museum, Bygdøy; p16 bl University of National
Antiquities, Uppsala, Sweden; p18 tr, p24 t&b, p26 bl
National Museum, Copenhagen.

Paul Windett courtesy of **Ydalir Vikings**: p12 bl, p20 bl,
p22 t&b. (www.ydlair.co.uk)

TAKE CARE
WHEN USING SCISSORS

Words in **bold** are explained
in the glossary on page 30.

PAINT A VIKING STONE

The Vikings painted stones to record their history and stories of gods and monsters. Make your own Viking stone in five easy steps.

YOU WILL NEED:
SMOOTH STONE OR PEBBLE • WASHING-UP BOWL • WASHING-UP LIQUID • CHALK OR WHITE PENCIL • ACRYLIC PAINTS • BRUSHES • GOLD METALLIC PEN • ACRYLIC VARNISH OR PVA MIXTURE (3 PARTS PVA, ONE PART WATER)

1

Find a smooth stone or pebble in the garden or park. Wash it in soapy water, rinse and leave to dry.

2

With a white pencil, carefully copy the picture on the opposite page onto your stone.

3

Paint the face blue, except for the eyes and mouth. Paint the mouth red and add a white dot on each side.

4

Paint the eyes light blue. Once all the paint is dry, use a gold metallic pen to go over your lines.

5

Use a clean brush to add a coat of PVA mixture as varnish. Leave to dry, then add another coat.

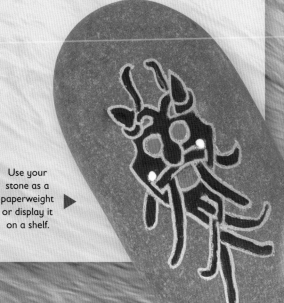

Use your stone as a paperweight or display it on a shelf. ▶

SURVIVAL SKILLS

The Vikings lived in the north of Europe, where the winters were long and snowy, and the summers were short. Families survived by growing oats and barley, and raising sheep, goats and cattle. They planted apple and plum trees, and created gardens to grow onions, peas and cabbages. In the summer, they cut grass and dried it to make hay for their animals to eat later in the year.

Viking homes were made of wood, stone or turf (slabs of earth with growing grass). Roofs were also made of turf, or they were thatched (covered with dried straw). This is a reconstruction of a Viking home, with modern windows!

DID YOU KNOW?

THE VIKINGS BURNED WHALE-OIL IN LAMPS, TO LIGHT THEIR HOMES, AND RUBBED BLUBBER (FAT) FROM SEALS INTO THEIR SHOES AND LEATHER WAISTCOATS TO MAKE THEM WATERPROOF.

FORAGING FOR FOOD

Most Viking families lived close to the sea. They went fishing and caught large sea-creatures, such as whales and seals. They hunted wild birds to eat, and wild animals, such as wolves, foxes and reindeer, for their skins and furs. They gathered shellfish, birds' eggs, wild mushrooms, nuts and berries. In the winter, when there were fewer animals to kill and nothing grew, Vikings went hungry and sometimes starved.

HOME AND HEARTH

A typical Viking house had thick walls to keep out the cold, and one big room where the family lived and slept. In the middle of the room, a fire was kept burning all the time, for warmth and for cooking. Viking homes were often smoky inside. Many houses had storerooms and work-rooms close by, together with barns for animals, called byres (say buy-ers).

Viking homes did not have much furniture apart from wooden tables, stools or benches, and storage chests. Women kept the keys to the chests.

MAKE A VIKING CHEST

Transform a shoe box into a chest for storing your treasures. Opening a chest without permission was a serious crime in Viking times.

1 Using a pair of compasses and a ruler, draw two semicircles that are the same width as your shoe box.

2 Extend the compass and around each semicircle, draw a slightly larger one. Cut out, around the larger semi-circles.

3 Cut in tabs. Draw a rectangle that's the same length as your shoe box and two and a half times its width.

4 Cut out the rectangle. Now glue a semicircle to each long edge of the the rectangle, a few tabs at a time.

5 Paint the shoe box and new lid. Add strips of gold card. Glue the overlap on the lid to the back of the shoe box.

Stick on a small square of gold card and draw on a key hole. Decorate the strips with a black marker pen.

RAIDERS FROM THE NORTH

This detail from the **Bayeux Tapestry** shows **Norman** warriors sailing their warships to invade England.

Vikings used the threat of raids to demand money from other nations. These payments were called 'Danegeld' (say dane-geld). If foreign kings refused to pay, Viking raiders attacked their lands. Each Viking king or jarl recruited local farmers to fight for him in his own private army called a lid (say lith). He expected them to be fiercely loyal to him, and to each other. In return, he rewarded them with treasures, and protected them from rival armies.

DID YOU KNOW?

VIKING RAIDERS CAPTURED PEOPLE AND THEN DEMANDED A RANSOM (BLOOD MONEY) TO FREE THEM ALIVE.

GOING BERSERK

Viking armies had troops of special wild warriors, called berserkers (say bear-ser-kerrs). They wore clothes made from bearskin, and believed the skins gave them magic powers. Before fighting, they worked themselves into a fury, howling and chewing their shields.

COURAGE AND CONVICTION

The Vikings admired strength and courage in both men and women. While men were away, Viking women ran the farms and defended family land from attackers. Many Viking raiders never came back – they were killed fighting or lost at sea. Viking people were expected to face death bravely. Viking poets said, 'Cattle die, families die, we ourselves must die.'

This helmet was designed to give extra protection to the wearer's eyes and nose. The crest on top helped guard his brain.

WEAR A JARL'S HELMET

Jarls wore strong metal helmets to protect their heads and scare their enemies. No one will recognize you behind this nose guard!

YOU WILL NEED:
BALLOON • OLD NEWSPAPER • PVA MIXTURE (3 PARTS PVA, ONE PART WATER) • SCISSORS • THICK CARD • PENCIL • CRAFT KNIFE • GLUE • PAINT AND BRUSHES

1

Blow up a balloon. Dip torn-up strips of newspaper into PVA mixture. Stick them to the top half of the balloon.

2

Build up several layers of papier-mâché strips. Leave to dry. (This may take several hours.)

3

Pop the balloon and remove it. Use scissors to trim the jagged edges straight, all the way round.

4

Draw the eye and nose piece onto card. Ask an adult to cut it out with a craft knife.

5

Glue the eye and nose piece to the papier-mâché helmet. When the glue is dry, paint the helmet gold.

If you want your helmet to shine, ask an adult to spray-paint it for you. Make sure they do it outside! ▶

DRAGON SHIPS

This 21.5m-long wooden ship has a snake-shaped **prow**. It was made in Norway over 1000 years ago.

Vikings lived in wild, harsh places. There were few roads or bridges, so it was difficult to travel overland. It was quicker and easier for Vikings to travel by boat – along rivers, around the coast or across the ocean. They made small, light boats for short coastal journeys and big boats called knarr (say naarr) with wide, deep **hulls** for longer voyages. Viking traders used knarr to carry goods overseas to sell. For raiding, the Vikings built fast, sleek warships. The biggest and best were called dragon ships, or drakkar (say drack-arr).

YOU WILL NEED:

TRACING PAPER • PENCIL • RULER • A1 SHEET CARD • BLACK AND WHITE PAINT • BRUSHES • CRAFT KNIFE

MAKE A DRAGON HEAD

Dragons appear in a lot of Viking art because they were fierce, wild and mysterious – just like famous Viking heroes.

A snarling magic beast, carved in wood. It was found in the ship above. Similar carvings were used on the prows of Viking warships.

1

Draw a grid of 2cm squares onto tracing paper. Put the grid over the dragon on the left. Draw round it.

3

Copy the contents of each square on the tracing paper grid into the matching square on the big grid.

BUILDING SHIPS

The largest Viking drakkar so far discovered is 30 metres long and 3.7 metres wide. Whatever their size, all Viking ships were built from overlapping wooden planks. These were fastened to a heavy oak **keel** (the 'backbone') with strong iron nails. Tall pine-tree trunks were used for **masts**, and a steering oar was fitted at the **stern**.

MASTER SEAFARERS

It took around 120 men, two to each oar, to row a big, fast drakkar. Viking ships were designed with streamlined hulls to skim over the waves, rather than ploughing through them. This made them less likely to fill with water and sink. The Vikings were proud of their ships, and gave them splendid names, such as 'Long Serpent'.

DID YOU KNOW?

IN WINTER, WHEN RIVERS, LAKES AND BOGS WERE FROZEN, VIKINGS TRAVELLED ON SLEDGES, SKATES AND SKIS.

Prop your dragon head up behind your bed or next to your bedroom door.
▼

2

On a card sheet, draw a large grid of 10 x 10cm squares. Both grids need the same number of squares.

4

Mix white and black paint to make grey. Paint your dragon head and leave it to dry completely.

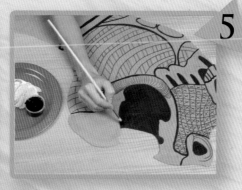

5

Ask an adult to cut out your dragon head. Draw on details, such as the eye. Go over with black paint.

11

WEAPONS AND ARMOUR

Viking battles were mostly fought on foot. Warriors leaped from their ships or lined up behind their leaders – then charged! Sometimes, they threw a single spear before attacking. They did this to show that they claimed all the men they were going to kill for the Viking war-god, Odin.

Viking warriors had to provide their own weapons and armour, or steal them on raids! The man on the left is wearing chain mail.

DID YOU KNOW?

KINGS HAD BLOOD-CURDLING NICKNAMES SUCH AS 'RUTHLESS', 'BLOODAXE', 'IRONSIDE', 'FLATNOSE' AND 'HAIRY-BREEKS' (WHICH MEANS HAIRY TROUSERS).

WEAPONS AT THE READY

Vikings fought using several different weapons, but their favourites were long, sharp swords and heavy battleaxes. They used these to hack, stab and bash their enemies at **close quarters**. Warriors also hurled spears and shot arrows from bows to attack enemies from a distance. Swords, axes, spear-tips and arrowheads were all crafted from iron. Bows and spear-shafts were made of wood. The best weapons were decorated with real gold and silver, and had names such as 'Stinger' and 'Leg Biter'.

Banners were carried on tall poles so that Viking warriors could see where their leaders were on the battlefield, and follow them.

DRESSED TO FIGHT

For protection in battle, ordinary Vikings wore tough leather caps and **tunics**. Kings, chiefs and other top warriors had iron helmets and chain-mail armour made from hundreds of iron rings linked together. Warriors carried circular shields made of wood and leather strengthened with iron. These guarded a warrior's body, from his shoulders to his knees.

Make a Battle Banner

Viking warriors carried banners high as they went into battle. Banners often had pictures of strong, fierce animals painted on them.

YOU WILL NEED:
A1 SHEET OF WHITE CARD • PENCIL • RULER • BLACK FELT-TIP PEN • BLUE AND WHITE PAINT • PAINTBRUSHES • SCISSORS • DOUBLE-SIDED STICKY TAPE • 1m LENGTH OF DOWEL

1

Draw a 58 x 44cm rectangle on card. Make a mark a third in from one long edge and halfway along.

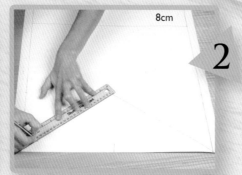

2

8cm

Join up the corners to the mark. Draw a vertical margin line 8cm in from the other long edge.

3

Draw eight equally spaced horizontal lines in the margin. Copy the boar from this page onto the banner.

4

Go over the boar, strips and edges in black felt-tip pen and paint the background blue.

5

Cut the banner out. Cut away every other strip down the margin. Fix the remaining strips around the dowel.

You could paint the back of your banner, too, so that it looks the same from both sides.

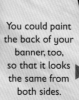

13

EXPLORERS AND SETTLERS

Settlers worked hard to build houses in new lands. They also built boats for fishing. ▶

Daring Viking explorers sailed vast distances across unknown seas and oceans. They were searching for new goods to trade and new lands to farm. Some also hoped to find new kingdoms to rule, away from their rivals in the Viking homelands.

DID YOU KNOW?

EXPLORERS KNEW THEY WERE NEAR LAND WHEN THEY SAW SEAWEED, ICEBERGS, BIRDS – OR SMELT SHEEP!

HEADING WEST

In 795 CE, Vikings from Norway headed west, to settle in Scotland and Ireland. Later, they reached Iceland (870 CE) and then Greenland (983 CE). From Greenland, they sailed across the Atlantic Ocean to Vinland (now Newfoundland, Canada), in around 1000 CE.

OTHER ADVENTURES

Around 750 CE, Swedish Vikings headed east, to set up forts and camps in Russia. From 860 CE, Vikings from Denmark began to settle in north and east England. They ruled a kingdom there until 1042 CE. Some settlers were women. For example, Aud the Deep-Minded was the wife and daughter of chiefs. She led her family to settle in Iceland around 880 CE.

◀ Ships carrying explorers and settlers had weather-vanes fitted to their masts or prows.

14

MAKE A WEATHER VANE

Vikings fitted weather vanes to their ships, to show which way the wind was blowing. Make a stunning weather vane from foil card.

YOU WILL NEED:
A4 TRACING PAPER • PENCIL • GOLD FOIL CARD • CRAFT KNIFE • CUTTING BOARD • FINE BLACK MARKER PEN

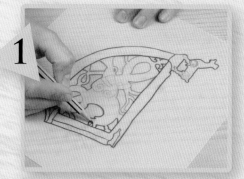

1

Copy the weather vane on page 14 onto tracing paper. Go over lightly first and then darken all your lines.

2

Transfer the tracing onto gold foil card. You'll have to press hard to make an impression.

3

Ask an adult to cut out your weather vane with a craft knife on a cutting board.

4

Use a fine black marker pen to add decoration around the edge and details to the horse.

You could attach your weather vane to a dowel rod with sticky tape. Alternatively, fix your weather vane to the window with adhesive putty. ▶

CRAFTS, MARKETS AND TOWNS

There were several large, rich trading towns in the Viking homelands. The most famous were Hedeby in Denmark, Birka in Sweden, York in England and Dublin in Ireland. These towns were planned, defended and owned by Viking kings. Highly skilled craftworkers lived and worked in towns, making fine iron weapons, gold and silver jewellery, delicate ivory combs, embroidered clothes and carved wooden furniture.

▲ Viking wood-carving showing a blacksmith (left) holding red-hot iron with tongs while he hammers it into shape. His helper (right) uses bellows to fan the fire that heats the iron.

YOU WILL NEED:
PAIR OF COMPASSES •
2 PLASTIC LIDS • STRING •
SCISSORS • DRINKING STRAW

MAKE A MERCHANT'S SCALES

Traders carried a small set of scales and weights with them to work out the value of coins from different lands.

▲ Scales used by a travelling merchant. The merchant would have held them in his hand, put silver coins in one pan, and little weights in the other. When the top bar was level, he could tell how much the coins weighed.

1

With the point of a compass, make four evenly spaced holes around the edge of each lid.

4

Cut a 25cm length of string. Tie the end to the knot above one lid. Then feed the string through the straw.

GOODS AND MERCHANTS

Travelling merchants visited Viking towns to sell luxuries from foreign lands. Rich Viking customers prized glass from Germany, wine from France and silk from Asia. Raiders also brought captives to towns, to sell as slaves. Viking slaves helped with ordinary tasks and some were taught craft skills. For example, they might spend all day, everyday, weaving wool.

THE LOCAL MARKET

At country markets, Viking farmers and their families **bartered** farm produce for other local goods, such as honey, wax, dried fish, wooden buckets, willow baskets, iron nails, amber beads and stout leather shoes. Coins were not widely used by ordinary Viking people. Sometimes hack-silver (silver scrap) was used for buying and selling, instead.

2

Cut eight 25cm lengths of string. Feed a length of string through each hole on both lids and knot.

3

On each lid, pull all four strings up to the same height and knot them together.

5

Pull string taut through straw and tie the end to the other lid's strings. Add a string handle and fix with sticky tape.

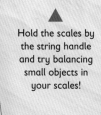

Hold the scales by the string handle and try balancing small objects in your scales!

17

CLOTHES AND JEWELLERY

The Vikings needed layers of warm clothing to protect them from winter weather and on long, cold sea voyages. They also wanted their clothes to look good. They enjoyed wearing embroidered cloth and heavy, metal jewellery to display their wealth and their **rank** in society.

Solid gold brooch (left), made for a very rich Viking leader and a heavy silver arm-ring, worn by a Viking warrior.

FABRIC AND FIBRE

Rich Vikings wore fine wool cloth, dyed in bright colours, or smooth silk and linen. They lined their clothes with fur and trimmed them with braid or embroidery. Poor people wore rough cloth, made from homespun wool or thick, hard-wearing linen. Viking craftswomen also spun and wove fibre from stinging nettles, which produced a soft, silky material.

This rich Viking man is wearing a cosy fur hat, a thick wool cloak and boots of fur-lined leather.

DID YOU KNOW?

VIKING MEN AND WOMEN BATHED AT LEAST ONCE A WEEK – USUALLY ON A SATURDAY – BY HAVING A SAUNA (A BATH IN CLOUDS OF STEAM). THIS AMAZED THE ENGLISH, WHO WASHED LESS OFTEN.

THE VIKING LOOK

Men wore a knee-length tunic, belted round the waist, over an under-shirt and baggy trousers. In cold weather, they added a thick cloak and a hat. Women wore a long under-dress with a pinafore-dress on top, held in place by brooches. In cold weather, they wrapped a big shawl round their shoulders. Married women usually wore a hood-like cap, over long hair tied up in a bun. Viking men, as well as women, wore eye-liner to draw attention to their eyes.

DYE MATERIAL THE VIKING WAY

Vikings used berries and vegetables to dye material beautiful colours. Their dyeing technique still works 1000 years later!

1

2

Chop the beetroot and put it in a saucepan half-filled with cold water. Remember to wear rubber gloves.

Put in the tape and T-shirt. Ask an adult to bring it to the boil. Simmer for 1 hour, stirring occasionally.

3

4

When cool, strain through a sieve. Then remove the tape and T-shirt from the beetroot pulp.

Rinse well and hang up to drip dry. Once the tape's dry, paint a Viking pattern along it.

5

Feel like a proud Viking, in your bright, patterned top. (Don't forget that your top is not colour-fast and should always be washed separately.) ▶

When the T-shirt and tape are dry, stick or sew the tape to the T-shirt.

19

FOOD AND DRINK

PRANDIVM: ET HIC EPISCOPVS CIBV ET POTV BE NE DIC IT.

Vikings ate two meals a day: early in the morning, and in the evening after the day's work was done. Usually, food was simple, but Vikings loved feasting on special occasions, such as Yule (the midwinter festival) or weddings.

Norman warriors feasting. You can see knives and platters on the table and two men holding drinking bowls (left).

DID YOU KNOW?

ONION PORRIDGE WAS GIVEN TO ANY WARRIOR WITH A STOMACH WOUND, THEN HIS INJURIES WERE SNIFFED. IF HIS CARERS COULD SMELL ONIONS, THEY KNEW THE MAN WOULD DIE.

FINE FARE

Meals were based on grains. Oats were boiled to make porridge while barley and rye were ground into flour, mixed with water, and baked as 'flat bread'. Vikings also liked meat and fish, stewed or spit-roasted. They made butter and cheese from milk, sausages from blood, and spicy relishes from mustard and garlic. In winter, Vikings ate thick vegetable stews, and warming soup made from dried peas. In summer, they loved to eat fresh fruit and wild woodland berries. They drank water, milk or ale brewed from barley.

USEFUL UTENSILS

Vikings ate from wooden platters or soapstone bowls. They cut and speared food with knives, or sipped from spoons carved from wood or sheep's horn. Poor people drank from wooden mugs or bowls. Rich people used glass or silver cups, or huge drinking horns. Viking women did the cooking, and preserved food to eat in the winter. They salted fish and meat, smoked them above cooking fires, and used ice, for deep-freezing.

Vikings made huge cups for drinking from animal horn. They could not be put down without spilling the contents, so they were only used at feasts and other special occasions.

DRINK VIKING APPLE JUICE

Warm, sweet apple juice wasn't only tasty, it kept out the cold! Make some, with a little help from an adult, and sup like a Viking!

1 Wash the apples. Ask an adult to remove the pips and cores, and chop the rest into thin slices.

2 Put the apple slices, cold water and a teaspoon of clear honey into a saucepan.

3 Ask an adult to heat the mixture, stirring well until it starts to boil. Then remove from the heat.

Before you drink, wish your friends 'Good Health!', just like a Viking would have done. ▶

4 Ask an adult to strain the mixture into a jug. Once it's cooled a little, pour some into a mug and drink!

21

SPORTS, GAMES AND MUSIC

The Vikings loved sport, board games and story-telling. Playing sport was a good way to show off strength, fitness and skill. Many sports were also excellent training for war. Viking summer games included swimming, wrestling, running, jumping, skating and weightlifting. In winter, Viking men and boys played games rather like ice hockey on frozen rivers and lakes. Vikings played to win, and competitors were often injured. They also liked to watch violent fights between animals, especially horses.

Viking wrestlers fought fiercely. The loser might end up badly hurt.

PLAY HNEF-TAFL

Hnef-tafl (say Neff-tah-fell) means 'king's table'. One player must protect the king from his opponent's much larger army!

YOU WILL NEED:
CORRUGATED CARD • PENCIL • RULER • RED AND BLACK FELT-TIP PENS • AIR-DRYING CLAY • MODELLING TOOL • 24 CHUNKY BLUE BEADS • 12 CHUNKY WHITE BEADS

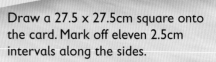

1 Draw a 27.5 x 27.5cm square onto the card. Mark off eleven 2.5cm intervals along the sides.

Board games were fun but they also helped Viking warriors learn how to plan battles and raids.

3 Design some Viking-style patterns on spare paper. Draw your best design onto each of the red squares.

22

INDOOR GAMES

Peaceful pastimes included board games, dice and knucklebones (played like 'jacks' today). Children played with toy boats, model horses, dolls, spinning tops and wooden weapons. Dancing, acrobatics and juggling – sometimes using knives! – were popular among Viking warriors.

AROUND THE FIRE

At feasts, and on long, dark, winter evenings, Viking families and their guests liked to sit round the fire, listening to music and story-telling. Songs and dances were played on harps, **lyres**, whistles and drums. Kings and chiefs paid poets to compose special songs that praised them. Professional entertainers travelled from village to village, **reciting** poems and telling stories.

DID YOU KNOW?

VIKINGS WERE FOND OF RIDDLES AND PROVERBS (WISE SAYINGS) SUCH AS 'GENEROUS AND BRAVE MEN GET THE BEST OUT OF LIFE'.

Set up your board like this before you start each game.

▼

2

Join up your marks to make a grid. Colour in the four corner squares and the square in the centre.

4

To make the king, shape a 2cm high cylinder from clay. Use a modelling tool to draw on his face and beard.

HOW TO PLAY

RULES FOR TWO PLAYERS

The white army's aim is to get the king safely to any of the four corners. The blue army's aim is to capture the king. The game is over when one army achieves its aim. You can move each piece horizontally or vertically as many squares as you wish but you must land on an empty square. Only the king can stop on the red squares. To capture an enemy counter, sandwich it between two of your pieces (see below) or between your piece and a corner square. You can take more than one piece in a go. The blue army starts!

EXAMPLE
If the black piece lands here, both white pieces have black pieces on either side. So, the white pieces are trapped and can be taken.

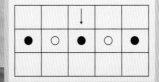

GODS AND HEROES

The Vikings **worshipped** many different gods and goddesses. Odin was the god of war. The Vikings believed that he could see into the future and was wise, cruel and mysterious. Kings and warriors asked him for protection. Thor, the thunder god, was strong but stupid. He fought giants, ruled the weather and protected farmers. Frey, and his sister, Freya (say Fray-yah), were generous and life-giving. Valkyries (say Val-keer-eez) were sky-goddesses, who flew high above battles. They collected the spirits of men who had died bravely and carried them off to warrior heaven called Valhalla (say Val-hal-lah).

◀ Little metal statue of the goddess Freya. Vikings said she made people, animals and plants grow strong and healthy.

DID YOU KNOW?

Some days of the week are still named after Viking gods, such as 'Thursday' which means 'Thor's day'.

SPIRITS, MONSTERS AND STORIES
Vikings believed in elves, giants, **trolls** and other nature spirits. They loved stories about gods, monsters, heroes and adventures. Many stories told how the whole world – including the gods – was destined to be destroyed at Ragnarok (say Rag-narr-ok), a terrible final battle.

PLEASING THE GODS
Belief in gods helped Vikings cope with their tough, difficult lives. They prayed to gods before going into battle or setting off on long journeys. They offered them food and drink, to ask for favours. In wooden temples, they offered the gods animal **sacrifices**.

▲ Viking men and women liked to carry amulets (lucky charms). Many were shaped like the magic hammer used by the god Thor when he fought giants and monsters.

24

MOULD THOR'S HAMMER

Viking blacksmiths poured molten metal into moulds to make objects in special shapes. You can do the same with plaster of Paris!

YOU WILL NEED:
NON-DRYING CLAY • RULER • MODELLING TOOLS • OLD PEN TOP • PLASTER OF PARIS MIXTURE (ALWAYS FOLLOW THE INSTRUCTIONS ON THE PACKET)

1 Shape non-drying clay into a small block. Press the sides against a ruler to make them smooth and straight.

2 With a modelling tool, scoop out the hammer shape. Be careful not to go through the bottom!

3 Press a pen top into the bottom of your mould to make circle patterns on your hammer.

4 Following the instructions on the packet, mix up the plaster of Paris. Pour it up to the top of the mould.

5 When the plaster of Paris has completely dried, carefully peel away the clay mould to reveal your amulet.

You could use gold or silver paint to make your amulet look like metal. ▶

BURIED TREASURES

The Vikings thought that when a person died, their spirit lived on. Warriors and unmarried girls went to live with Odin and Freya in the sky. Old or sick people went to a cold kingdom ruled by Hel, a gloomy, scary goddess. Ordinary peoples' spirits stayed close to their graves – and sometimes haunted the living.

READY FOR THE NEXT LIFE
In early Viking times, dead bodies were burned. Vikings thought the fires set dead peoples' spirits free from their bodies. Before burning, dead people were given everything they might need in the next world, such as clothes, weapons, jewellery and food. Sometimes slaves were killed, to serve their owners after death. After burning, dead peoples' ashes were scattered or buried in pottery jars.

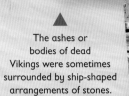

The ashes or bodies of dead Vikings were sometimes surrounded by ship-shaped arrangements of stones.

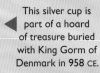

This silver cup is part of a hoard of treasure buried with King Gorm of Denmark in 958 CE.

DID YOU KNOW?
VIKINGS BURIED TREASURE TO KEEP IT SAFE BUT THEY OFTEN DIED OR WERE KILLED BEFORE THEY COULD DIG IT UP AGAIN. MANY OF THESE HOARDS HAVE BEEN FOUND LONG AFTER VIKING TIMES.

MESSAGES FROM THE PAST
After around 850 CE, most Viking dead bodies were not burned. Important people were buried in real ships, or ship-shaped wooden coffins. Everyone else was buried in holes in the ground. Many of the objects buried in these graves have survived until today. **Archaeologists** have discovered a lot about Viking ideas, designs and skills from grave goods.

MAKE GORM'S CUP

Make a Viking King's silver cup. Imagine being a Viking silversmith as you create patterns by pressing down into the foil.

1

Cut out three foil rectangles that will fit round your cup. Use double-sided sticky tape to stick them together.

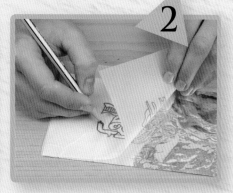

2

Copy the design on page 26 onto tracing paper. Put it on the foil. With a blunt pencil, press over each line.

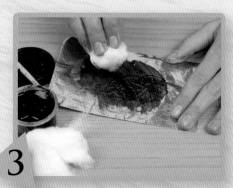

3

Rub black poster paint over the foil. Now gently wipe it away with clean cotton wool.

4

Trim the plastic cup down so that it's slightly shorter than the height of your foil drawing.

5

Wrap the foil around the cup and fix at the back with sticky tape. Fold excess foil in around the rim.

You can't drink from Gorm's cup but you could keep pens and pencils in it. ▶

27

PICTURE STONES AND RUNES

The Vikings used an ancient system of writing, called runes. Each letter was made of straight and diagonal lines because these were easier to carve into stone or wood than curves. Over 2500 Viking **inscriptions** in runes have survived. Some are labels, to show who owned an object. Some are letters or messages. Some are magic spells. Many of the finest are carved on tall stones. These were put up by families to remember people who had died, or by proud individuals who wanted to boast about their own achievements. Some stones only have runic writing while others are carved with pictures from Viking myths and legends.

A Viking picture stone. It has pictures of two snakes (top) and two dragons, with writing in runes around the outer edge.

A Viking carved the runic alphabet into this piece of pine. It also has magical messages carved on the back.

WRITE YOUR NAME IN RUNES

Find out what your name looks like in runes and then write it into soft balsa wood or card. Why not make one as a present for a friend, too?

YOU WILL NEED:
PIECE OF BALSA WOOD OR THICK CARD • PENCIL • PAPER • BLACK FELT-TIP PEN • WOOL • STICKY TAPE

1

Using the chart opposite, find and write down the runes that stand for the letters of your name.

OLD, OLD STORIES

Historians do not know how many Viking people could read and write runes. Stories were passed on by word of mouth from older to younger people, and safely remembered for hundreds of years. Long after Viking times, scholars began to write down all the old Viking histories, adventures and poems. They called Viking stories 'sagas' (say sah-gaz) and their poems 'eddas' (say edd-ahz).

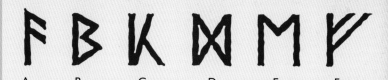

A	B	C	D	E	F

G	H	I	J	K	L	M

N	O	P	Q	R	S

T	U	V	W	X	Y	Z

DID YOU KNOW?

IMPORTANT PEOPLE PAID POETS CALLED SKALDS (SAY SKALLDZZ) TO SING POEMS PRAISING THEMSELVES AND THEIR GUESTS.

Hang your Viking name sign on your bedroom door.

2

Draw each rune onto the balsa wood or card. Use a pencil and press hard as you draw.

3

With a felt-tip pen, go over each of your runes. Then attach a loop of wool to the back with sticky tape.

29

GLOSSARY

archaeologist Someone who studies the past by digging up ancient objects or bones.

barter To exchange goods for others of equal value.

Bayeux Tapestry A 70 metre-long embroidered cloth showing the battle of Hastings, which took place in England, in 1066 CE.

close quarters Very near.

hull The hollow, lower part of a ship.

inscription Writing carved into wood or stone.

jarl A Viking nobleman and war-leader.

keel A long, strong piece of wood that acts like a backbone in a ship's hull.

lyre A musical instrument with strings, like a small harp.

mast A tall pole that holds up a ship's sails.

merchant Trader.

Norman A Viking whose family had settled in northern France.

prow The front end of a ship.

rank A person's place in society.

reciting Repeating from memory.

sacrifice A person or animal who is killed to please the gods.

settler Person who leaves their home to live in a new land.

stern Back end of a ship.

troll Small, cruel, cunning Viking monster with a long beard. Vikings said that trolls attacked travellers.

tunic Long, straight piece of clothing with no sleeves.

worship To respect and love a god or goddess.

INDEX

NOTES FOR PARENTS AND TEACHERS

• Research Viking myths and legends about the creation of the world, from library books or a website such as http://www.cdli.ca/CITE/v_creation. htm. Discuss the story with the children, and then help them to plan and make a picture book, retelling the creation myth. This could be a group project, with each child responsible for a different episode in the story.

• Viking musicians played lyres (harps), handbells, animal-horn trumpets and whistles made of bone, accompanied by wooden clappers or hand-clapping. Listen to an ancient Viking song 'Drømde mig en drøm' ('I dreamed a dream last night') played on a lyre at http:// www.vikinganswerlady.com/music. shtml#Reconstruction. Help the children to learn to play this tune, and to write their own songs on a dream theme.

• The Vikings loved nicknames. These were often funny, but could also be very revealing about an individual's appearance or character. Ask the children to invent nicknames they'd like to have for themselves, or to draw cartoon characters illustrating some real Viking nicknames. You can find a list at http://www.regia.org/members/names.htm#VikF

• With the children, find out more about Viking ships and make a big map to show where the Vikings sailed. You could decorate the map with cut-outs of different Viking ships, sea-creatures and sea monsters like the famous Kraken (giant squid). For pictures of Viking ships, see http://www.khm.uio. no/english/viking_ship_museum/ and http://www.copenhagenpictures.dk/ vik_skib.html. For a virtual Viking voyage online, and much more, see: http://www. mnh.si.edu/vikings/start.html.

• Simple Viking jewellery is fun and easy to make. The children could string coloured glass beads on a cord to make a Viking-style necklace (see, for example, http://www.gov.im/mnh/collections/ archaeology/vikings/paganlady.xml). Or they could trace wavy Viking patterns from a book onto a strip of card or leather to make a Viking wristband.

Useful websites
Try this helpful site, with information, quizzes and activities, supported by the Norwegian Ministry of Education: http:// www.viking.no/. It welcomes visitors with a charming Viking 'greeting' poem, which would be easy for most children to learn.

Simple information for children, and a great many links (some for adults, some for children) can be found at http:// worldhistory.mrdonn.org/vikings.html.

To see a list of Viking reenactment groups visit http://www.clash-of-steel. co.uk/pages/links_groups.php?cat=Viking

Introduction

WHAT ARE YOU WEARING today? Are you a slave to fashion, buying catwalk styles as soon as they make it to the high street? Maybe you go your own way, mixing and matching individual clothes to create a look that's entirely original. Or do you shun fashion altogether, and just wear black?

However outrageous your style, you'll have trouble matching the most extreme fashions from the past, or from around the world. Are you into piercings? How about wearing a plate the size of a saucer in your lip? Or if high heels are your thing, maybe you'd like to totter around on the 75-cm (30-in) monsters popular in 16th century Venice?

In this book, you can read about these fashions, and many more that you won't want to imitate. If some sound appealing, be wary of copying them. A waist you can wrap your hands around might turn a few heads, but you'd have to risk breaking some ribs to achieve it!

Would You Believe...?

When, where, who, which, what? When was there a fine for wearing fur? Whereabouts in the world did 600 women use makeup to kill their husbands? Who made the first bras? Which women had the tiniest waists? What fabric was worth more than gold? If you want to find out the answers, read on!

Fashionable Figures

S TARING DOWN from billboards or gazing from glossy magazines, fashion models are sometimes hard to tell apart. Always tall, thin and tanned, they challenge us to lose weight so we can squeeze into ever smaller clothes. But it wasn't always like this. Ancient people had very different ideas of beauty.

Would You Believe...?

Fantastic fat
Not everyone agrees with the "thin is beautiful" idea. In southern Nigeria, fat is traditionally attractive: brides-to-be spent months in "fattening rooms" eating to gain weight. The stars of India's Bollywood movies were plump, too – until recently, when Western movies made thin fashionable.

For Stone-Age folk, fat was fantastic! The statues they created show bulging bodies. In a world where food was scarce – and there was a risk that tonight's dinner might bite its hunters – being thin meant being sick or weak.

▲ **Stone-Age good looks**
Created about 6,000 years ago, this fist-sized pottery figure shows that Stone-Age artists admired shapely women who could provide many healthy babies. The "sleeping lady" came from the cave temple of Hal Saflieni, discovered in 1902 on the Mediterranean island of Malta.

Studying paintings at an art gallery, or leafing through a vintage magazine to look at the photographs, shows that the obsession with being thin is surprisingly new.

Artists like 16th-century Flemish painter Rubens show women as plump, happy and attractive

Hourglass

In the 1950s, the perfect figure was an "8" – not a size eight, but a small waist between a bulgy bottom and top. Thin meant fashionable only from the 1980s. Stick-like thinness is unhealthy, though: the truly trendy balance good looks with sensible eating.

Fuller film star ▶
American movie star Jayne Mansfield showed that plump was glamorous. She wowed movie audiences in the mid-1950s with her generous figure.

▲ **Skinny chic**
Fashion photos for designer Calvin Klein made English model Kate Mos[s] famous in the 1990s. Her extreme thinness made it fashionable to loo[k] like a waif (a starved young girl.) Women have to endure permanen[t] hunger and risk potentially dangerous diets to achieve this loo[k]

Ancient World

S WELTERING IN the dusty desert heat of the Nile Valley, women in ancient Egypt had a hard time looking smart. To keep their draped see-through linen dresses beautifully crisp and clean, wealthy Egyptians swapped them as often as four times a day.

Rich and poor

Egyptian fashions changed slowly, but women and men showed off their wealth and style with collars, bangles and belts of gold and precious stone. Poorer folk wore simpler jewellery made of colourful pottery beads.

▼ Perfume cones
In Egyptian paintings men and women are often shown wearing "perfume cones" on their wigs. But nobody has ever found one: artists may have drawn the shape to show that the wig was scented.

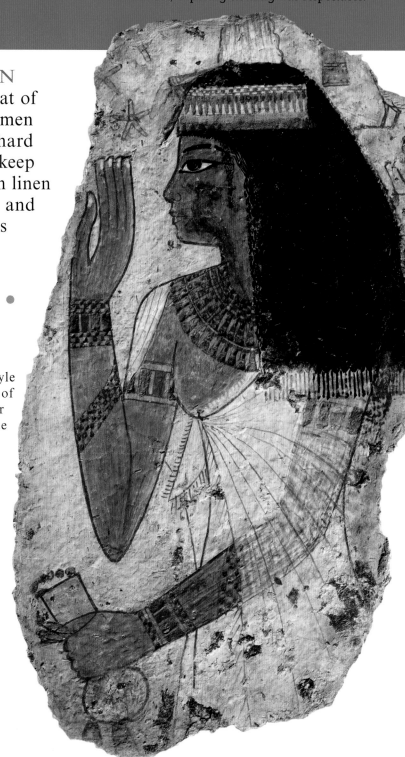

In ancient Greece and Rome, getting dressed meant winding yourself in lengths of fabric. Pins and weights held them in place. Styles rarely changed, but fashionable women did not dare to wear last season's colours.

▼ **Ancient Rome**
The *stola* worn by Roman women was made from cotton, silk or wool. It covered the whole body and, in public, respectable women covered their heads, too. One Roman citizen, Sulpicius Gallus, even divorced his wife because she left the house with her head uncovered.

Most Egyptian men wore pleated skirts

◄ **Ancient Greece**
Ancient Greek men and women dressed in garments called *chitons*: long lengths of fabric draped over the shoulders and tied around the waist. This statue from the 4th century BCE shows a woman wearing a cloak called a *himation* over her *chiton*.

Would You Believe...? Would You Believe...?

Costly clothing
Purple silk was the ultimate fashion fabric in ancient Rome. Silk was imported all the way from distant Asia, and was worth its weight in gold. The purple used to dye it was 20 times more costly. It was made from sea snails: 10,000 of them made enough dye to colour one garment.

One Roman fabric was made to look like clotted blood – it was black, but sparkled in sunlight

Forbidden Fashions

WOULD YOU pay a fine for wearing a silk hat, a gold ring or a lace collar? If you had lived six centuries ago, you might have had no choice! Special rules, called sumptuary (spending) laws, controlled who could wear luxurious clothes and who had to dress in boring wool.

Sumptuary laws made sure that ordinary people did not look like noble men and women – those people whose families ruled the land. The laws also aimed to limit the amount of costly goods brought in from abroad, because buying them harmed the nation's trade.

Peasantly fashionable ▶
The poor people who grew crops to feed their rich, well-dressed masters had to wear woollen clothes, either undyed or in dull shades. English farm workers wore traditional clothes in these colours until the early 20th century.

Knights and merchants

King Edward III ruled in 1337 that nobody less important than a knight could wear fur (he later let merchants wear it – if they were five times richer than knights!). Sumptuary laws soon ended, but they set styles for working people's clothes until just a century ago.

In the 17th century, foreign lace was completely banned in France

▲ **Jewels and gems**
Bans on buttons seem strange now, but in the 14th century buttons were often carved from precious stones. These Chinese buttons are made of jade, which only nobles were allowed to wear.

Coronation costumes ▶
The clothes worn by England's royal family on special occasions are rich in materials once controlled by sumptuary laws. This crowning dress has a trim of ermine fur, which nobody below a lord could wear.

GARB BANS

FLORENCE, 1322
Silk and scarlet clothes can only be worn in the home.

ENGLAND, 1362
Yeomen and below cannot wear silk, silver, chains, jewels or buttons.

PERUGIA, ITALY, 1366
Velvet, silk and satin are banned.

FRANCE, 1583
Only princes can wear jewels and pearls on their clothes; gold and silver embroidery are banned.

CHINA, 1680s
Yellow clothes are banned for all except the emperor's friends and family.

Smooth Operator

BY SHAVING, scraping, waxing or plucking, women since ancient times have tried to make their skin as smooth and hairless as polished marble. Most men shared their pain, cutting their chins daily with blades of stone or bronze.

In ancient China, dancers desperate for smooth skin once removed hair with *rhusma* – burning quicklime mixed with poisonous arsenic. Later generations played safe with painful pumice or tweezers.

▲ **Shaving stone**
Pumice stone, thrown out by erupting volcanoes, was one of the first razors. Its rough surface can be used to scrape off hair. English writer Samuel Pepys recorded in his diary for May 25th, 1662, that pumice shaved him "easily, speedily and cleanly".

Sugar solution ▶
Sugaring is a way to get rid of hair, first used in ancient Egypt and still popular today. A sticky solution of sugar, lemon juice and water is pressed on to the skin, then stripped away – removing the hair at the root.

Hairless and holy
Ancient Egyptian people thought that hair was unclean. Men shaved their faces, and both sexes shaved their heads and wore wigs. Priests were the smoothest of all: to purify themselves before entering the temple they shaved off all their head and body hair, including their eyebrows!

Medieval Christians once saw beards as ungodly

In 1915, advertisements first featured women with shaved armpits. The lie that hair was unhealthy made smooth skin fashionable. Since then, sales of waxes, creams and razors have never stopped growing – just like the hair they briefly remove.

◀ **Sharp as a scalpel**
Cave paintings show Stone-Age men without beards: the flint blades they shaved with were as sharp as modern razors. When men learned how to make tools from metal, bronze razors like these replaced stone blades, but they were not as sharp.

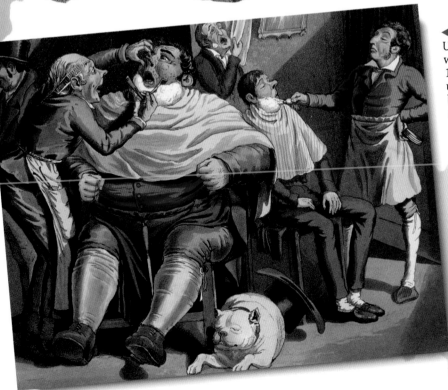

◀ **Sunday shave**
Until "safety razors" were invented in 1762, men shaved using sharp, straight blades. These were called "cut-throat" razors because, used carelessly, they could do exactly that. Many men preferred to trust the work of shaving to a barber rather than risk wounding themselves, as this humorous picture makes clear.

Fashion
Victims

CHECKING THE MIRROR, a fashion victim primps and pouts, adjusts a feather or two, then steps out – on to the battlefield. It isn't just catwalk queens who follow fashion: when soldiers from the past went to war they literally dressed to kill!

Practical yet stylish
Until the 17th century, European soldiers wore whatever they liked, but this made it hard to tell friend from foe in chaotic battles. Uniforms made a target of anyone in clothes that didn't match your own.

▲ French fashions
Medieval knights spent freely on fashions: styles in armour changed quickly, and a new steel suit cost as much as a car does today. Parade armour was the most elaborate. Never intended for battle, it was decorated with brilliant colours, gold and silver.

Samurai armour ▶
Japanese noblemen called samurai fought from the 12th to the 19th century in armour made of beautifully varnished metal and bamboo. They fixed coloured flags to their backs to identify themselves on the battlefield. Some wore elaborate helmets decorated with paper and leather nearly a metre (3 ft) high or wide.

The red coats of British soldiers made them stand out clearly in the sights of their foe's rifles

17th-century European officers used their uniforms to show off their wealth, adding rich embroidery, feathers and gold. Armies became a glittering mass of colour. This fashion parade ended in about 1890, when new uniforms in drab colours made soldiers harder to spot and shoot.

◄ **Emperor's finery**
Soldiers' uniforms were at their colourful best at the start of the 19th century. French emperor Napoleon, shown here, looked magnificent in gold buttons and trimmings. Even ordinary cavalry uniforms were made by the best Paris tailors and cost the equivalent of £1,500.

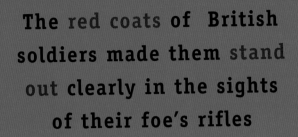

If You've Got it, Flaunt it

HOW LOW CAN YOU GO? When it comes to necklines, nobody went lower than the ancient Greeks. They worshipped women who wore tops that completely exposed their breasts. Ever since, women have tussled with "tut-tutters" in a battle over what it is decent to reveal.

It's not just the bust that causes a stir. Catwalk fashion models hide nothing, but even a glimpse of a woman's ankle can be shocking to some people. What you show is less important than where and when you show it. What's decent on the beach will raise eyebrows in a shopping centre!

● ● ● ● ● ● ● ● ● ● ●

◀ **Bare-breasted fashion**
Minoan women from the Mediterranean island of Crete may have worn costumes that showed off their shapely breasts. This picture is based on a pottery figure made 3,600 years ago for a religious ceremony. Minoan women were men's equals, and even took part in sports such as boxing and bull-leaping.

The careful 50s ▶

Screen heroine Marilyn Monroe reveals almost all that was respectable on the beach in the 1950s. Yet just ten years after this picture was taken, American fashion designer Rudi Gernreich introduced the first topless swimsuits. They caused outrage, but topless dresses followed not long after.

Miniskirts got shorter **in the 1960s as women's liberation moved on: by 1967, they** barely covered the bottom

Keeping it covered ▶

For much of the 19th century, Western women's fashions covered the whole body, often concealing even the neck and ankles. Although exposed flesh was considered shocking, the same was not true of a woman's shape. Figure-hugging dresses showed off women's curves.

◄ Roman style

Roman women's hair was piled so high that one writer joked that the women looked taller from the front than the back. To show off their wealth, women crowned their cones of curls with golden tiaras set with precious stones.

Miss Beehive

BIG HAIR BEGAN IN ANCIENT ROME. Wealthy women employed an *ornatrix* to arrange their hair into high, wobbling piles. Women's hair did not reach the same heights again until the 18th century. Then topknots towered so high that they sometimes touched candles hung from the ceiling, and caught fire!

▲ High-rise hair

The huge hair creations of the 18th century were constructed on high frames. Besides false hair, they sometimes included flowers, feathers or even model ships. The sculptures were expected to last three weeks before they needed rebuilding.

● ● ● ● ● ● ● ● ● ● ● ● ● ●

Geisha hair ►

Perfect hair was essential for Japan's geisha girls (traditional artist-entertainers). Starting in the 17th century, they combed up their hair into a style called *shimada*. The shiny black hair contrasted brilliantly with the geishas' white face makeup.

The beehive ▼
This high-piled style was named after dome-shaped beehives made from coiled rope. The aerosol hairspray that made it possible was invented in 1948. Made from varnish, the spray left the hair hard and sticky, and it was impossible to wash out.

Big hair was back in fashion in the 1950s, thanks to the invention of hairspray, which held tall styles in place. Men used greasy creams to sculpt "quiffs" that rolled over their foreheads like breaking waves. Big hair came back again in the 1980s, when styling gel made possible towering "Mohicans" and punky spikes in lurid colours.

Would You Believe...? Would You Believe...?

Horns of hair
Princesses of Tibet wore their hair sculpted into wide horns. Their maids wound their hair around light wooden sticks that stuck out 40 cm (14 in) on either side of their heads. The head-dresses stayed in place all the time, and stopped the princesses from turning their heads while asleep.

A Hat for all Occasions

IF HATS DID NOTHING but keep off the sun and rain, most of us would only rarely need them. But hats do much more than this. They can tell the world who we are; how rich, fashionable or important we are; and whether we are working or playing.

Hats pass on these messages because they are hard to miss when someone looks at us. And wearing the same hat as a big group of people suggests that we are all in the same club or clan.

The more beautiful the ladies, the higher were the steeples on their heads

▲ **High hats**
French and German women's hats reached a towering peak in the 15th century with a style called the "henin" or "steeple". The veil that hung from the tip sometimes fell to the waist. When it became fashionable for these giant hats to hide all the hair, women plucked or shaved their foreheads.

▲ **Tricorne hat**
Men had worn hats with the brim cocked (turned up) in earlier times, but in the 18th century it became fashionable to cock three sides, creating a three-cornered or "tricorne" hat. The hats were for carrying and posing only – they soon fell off their owners' huge wigs.

Would You Believe...?

Poor beaver
In the 17th century, the best material for making men's felt hats was beaver fur. This was so scarce that a good beaver hat cost a labourer four month's wages and a maid one year's wages. Nations fought wars for the best beaver land, and trapping made beavers almost extinct in Europe.

Hat fashions ▶
Bowler, top and Panama hats were fashionable in the early 20th century. The bowler (left) was for everyday wear, the top hat (middle) for formal events like weddings, and the Panama (right) for holidays.

Ascot ▼
Each year on Ladies Day at Britain's Ascot racecourse, women wear the most outrageous hats. The hats often make more news than the racing.

Why wear a hat?

At first, hats were certainly made for protection – against the weather, accidents or enemy blows. They do the same job today, but for most of us a hat is a bit of fun or the finishing touch for a fabulous outfit.

Monstrosities of 1827 ▼
Hats have often been an excuse for wild and weird decoration. This cartoon from 1827 makes fun of the hats by contrasting them with their owners' tightly squeezed waists.

Victorian women used long hat-pins to defend themselves against pestering men

Wild and
Untamed

I N THE LONG GRASS OF ITS
south Asian homelands, the tiger's stripes
are a perfect camouflage. They make this
elegant and powerful cat almost invisible.
On the back of a wealthy woman, a tiger
skin does the opposite, making her
stand out as cruel, selfish and caring
nothing for the natural world.

Dressing in "exotic" furs,
feathers and ivory used to
be the fashionable way of
showing off wealth and
status. Now it's a crime,
because hunting threatens
to wipe out some of the
world's most rare and
beautiful animals. A century
ago, there were probably
100,000 tigers. Fewer than
5,000 survive today.

▲ Pet trade
Furriers (tailors who make
clothes from fur) can
legally use cat and dog
skins in Europe (but not
in the USA). Some
animal welfare
organisations
believe the trade
in pet fur is
cruel, and are
campaigning
to stop it.

Fur coat ▶
Since humans first hunted,
they have valued fur for its
warmth, softness and beauty.
In 1954, when this picture was
taken, there seemed nothing
wrong with wearing a coat
made of leopard skins. The
growth of the environmental
("green") movement in the
1970s changed people's views.

In 2004, Tibetan customs officers **found the skins of 31 tigers and 581 leopards in a single lorry**

Illegal trade

Since 1975, the Convention on International Trade in Endangered Species (CITES) has banned the sale of skins and other parts of endangered animals.

▼ Big cats

The beautiful skin of the big cats makes them the most prized of all fur animals. They are at risk not only because of hunting, but also because the growth of cities, roads and farms means they have fewer places to live.

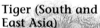
Tiger (South and East Asia)

Ocelot (South and Central America)

Jaguar (South and Central America)

◄ Prized plumes
The colourful feathers of birds of paradise once decorated hats. Hunting the birds stopped when it became clear that they were endangered. But today they are threatened once again, as loggers clear their forest homes in New Guinea.

Anti-fur protests

For some animal lovers, CITES does not go far enough. They believe farming animals for their skin is cruel. Their noisy protests have stopped many fashion designers from using real fur.

▲ Faking it
Nobody need wear real fur or skins. Manufacturers can create convincing look-alike materials with artificial fibres. However, furriers point out that real fur from farmed animals is "greener". Unlike fun fur, it rots when thrown away, and comes from a renewable source.

21

▼ **Slimline silhouette**
World War I (1914–1918) made women realise they were men's equals. They did the jobs of millions of men who had gone to Europe to fight. When the war was over, women showed off their new-found equality by dressing like men. The "flappers" of the 1920s cut their hair short and wore clothes that made them look flat-chested.

Bras and Bindings

BIG BUSTS OR SMALL? Fashion decides the shape, but it's a brassiere that provides it. Simple bras began in ancient Greece, with the *apodesme* – a rolled strip of cloth that lifted and supported the breasts. Roman women hid their breasts, binding them in a soft leather *mamilare*.

● ● ● ● ● ● ● ● ● ● ● ● ● ● ● ● ● ●

The modern brassiere started out in the UK under the name "bust girdle", sold by the Jaeger fashion house in 1904. It was given its modern name seven years later in the USA.

Would You Believe...?

Cantilevered bra
When Jane Russell was filming *The Outlaw*, the film's millionaire director Howard Hughes was unhappy with her costume. A keen pilot, he used aviation technology to design a special seamless bra with extra support. Unknown to Hughes, Russell never wore it because it was too uncomfortable.

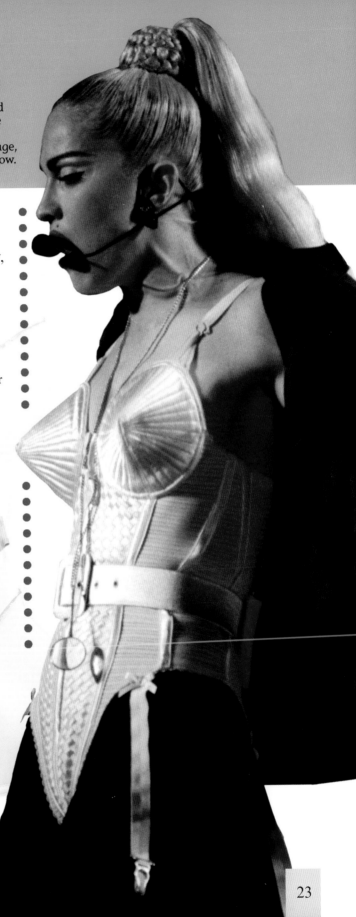

Cones on top ▶
Madonna put her bra centre stage on her 1990 "Blond Ambition" tour, flaunting it as a fashion garment and inspiring millions of imitations. Designed by Jean-Paul Gaultier, the cone-shaped cups copied and exaggerated the fashions of the 1950s, turning underwear into outer-wear. As planned, Madonna's outfit and act caused outrage, and the Pope called for people to boycott her show.

Fashion in bras alternates between the Greek and Roman shapes, either flaunting or hiding the breasts. Today, bras are the most complicated of all garments: some are made by hand from more than 20 pieces of fabric.

▼ Push-up revolution
Underwear that makes the cleavage look bigger is nothing new – it was popular in the 18th century. But the modern version is a lot more comfortable. Stretch fabrics and padding provide support, and new microfibre fabrics give bras a super-soft feel.

Busts swell when business booms: flat chests are fashionable in hard times

23

Crinolines
and Bustles

▲ 18th-century paniers (meaning "bread baskets") were worn to spread dresses width-ways.

I N A DRESS THE SIZE of a small tent, how would you get through a door or sit on a chair? Wealthy women in the 16th century had to find ways to do these things because, beneath their skirts, they wore hooped frames called farthingales to spread out the fabric.

Wealthy 16th-century women lived leisurely lives but, when the fashion for hooped dresses returned with crinolines in 1850, women of all classes wore them.

◄ Farthingales
The fashion for farthingales came from 15th-century Spain, where dressmakers used rope, woven grass, willow or whale bone to stiffen skirts. By the early 1600s, fashionable women were lifting and spreading their skirts with hoops the shape and size of cartwheels.

Beastly bustles ►
Victorian women padded out the backs of their skirts with huge and ridiculous devices called bustles. Some bustles were so wide and flat people joked that you could safely stand a tray of tea-cups on them.

▲ Crinolines
This humorous print shows just one of the problems that crinolines caused. Hoops of springy steel made going through doors and gates possible. But, as crinolines billowed to 180 cm (6 feet) across, women who tripped over could not even get up without help.

● ●

In factories, swirling crinolines caught in machines; in fields, mud and rain clung to farm girls' impractical hooped skirts. The fashion didn't last long: within 20 years, the crinoline had given way to the bustle, which exaggerated the shape and size of womens' bottoms. To this day, bustles and hoops are still worn to fill out fancy wedding dresses.

Would You Believe...?

Special chairs
Crinolines changed the shape, not only of the women who wore them, but of furniture, too. Sitting in a crinoline was tricky: all too often the front sprang up. Special chairs with short legs and a sloping back left extra space for the yards of spreading fabric, and solved the problem.

Farthingales were the most inconvenient and uncomfortable garments in history

Scaling down
Bustles changed from the 1860s, when they began to replace crinolines, through to their disappearance by 1890.

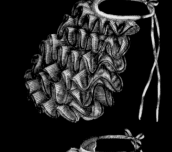

Construction ▲
Bustles started as "bum-rolls" – cushions tied above the hips to make a dress look fuller. Sprung steel hoops were introduced to make bustles lighter, but the smaller, later bustles got their fullness from layers of pleated fabric.

Waists like Wasps

◄ Wasps have a narrow waist.

This corset is for ► a 1-year-old child.

YOU CAN'T BREATHE. YOU CAN'T walk. You can't sit down. A tightly-laced corset may make your waist look tiny, but wearing one can be torture. Corsets are toughened, stiffened underwear. They are designed to squeeze the body into fashionable, often unnatural, shapes.

Invented 4,000 years ago in ancient Greece, corsets went to the extreme at the end of the 19th century, when the fashion was for figures that resembled an hourglass or a wasp.

▲ **Child-sized**
Children's bones are soft and bendy, so adults believed that the younger they put their daughters in corsets, the less harm it would do. Underwear manufacturers usually recommended child-sized corsets, not for their slimming effect, but as a way of keeping a child's back straight.

◄ **Menswear**
Men wore corsets to slim their waists and padding to emphasise other parts, as shown in this 1819 cartoon. The two servants dressing this "dandy" (fashionable man) are pulling on the laces that tighten his corset.

Not just for ladies
Beneath their starched shirts, some 19th-century men wore corsets to flatten their bulging stomachs. British prime minister Benjamin Disraeli wore one, and rivals of American president Martin van Buren claimed that he did, too.

Would You Believe...? Would You Believe...?

Fatal contraction
Corsets affected the health of millions, and occasionally even killed those who wore them. In 1859, a French woman died three days after going to a ball sporting a very narrow waist. An examination of her body showed that her corset had snapped three ribs, forcing them into her liver.

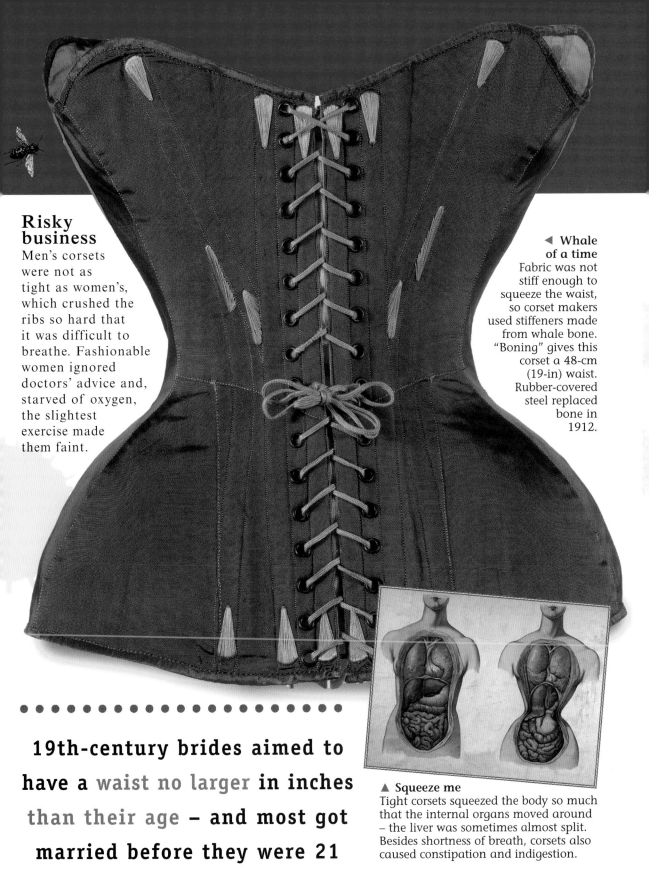

Risky business

Men's corsets were not as tight as women's, which crushed the ribs so hard that it was difficult to breathe. Fashionable women ignored doctors' advice and, starved of oxygen, the slightest exercise made them faint.

◄ Whale of a time
Fabric was not stiff enough to squeeze the waist, so corset makers used stiffeners made from whale bone. "Boning" gives this corset a 48-cm (19-in) waist. Rubber-covered steel replaced bone in 1912.

19th-century brides aimed to have a waist no larger in inches than their age – and most got married before they were 21

▲ Squeeze me
Tight corsets squeezed the body so much that the internal organs moved around – the liver was sometimes almost split. Besides shortness of breath, corsets also caused constipation and indigestion.

Squeezing and Shaping

▼ **Cradleboards**
Native Americans carried their children tied to cradleboards like this one. The board flattened the back of the skull. People in the Northwest went further, using boards that also pressed the child's forehead. The peaked shape this produced was a sign of beauty.

YOU'RE NEVER TOO young to start thinking about fashion and beauty – if you want a flat forehead, tiny feet or a neck like a giraffe. Children's bones are so flexible that, by binding and pressing, parents have literally squeezed their children into the shapes they wanted.

The aim of this body-bending was to make children more beautiful. The families that did it lived mostly in times or places where ideas of beauty were very different from our own. What now seems cruel was normal in 18th century China or America.

Small is beautiful

Wealthy Chinese people began tightly bandaging the feet of their infant daughters more than 1,000 years ago. As the girls grew up, the bindings broke their toes and deformed their feet, causing terrible pain. Binding a girl's feet showed how well off her family was: she was crippled, so she could neither walk nor work.

◄ **Small slippers**
Women with bound feet slipped them into unbelievably small shoes: some measuring just 10 cm (4 in) from heel to toe. As walking was almost impossible, the shoes got very little wear and were made of fine materials – the set shown here are silk. Foot-binding in China ended in 1911 after the country's revolution gave women more rights and freedom.

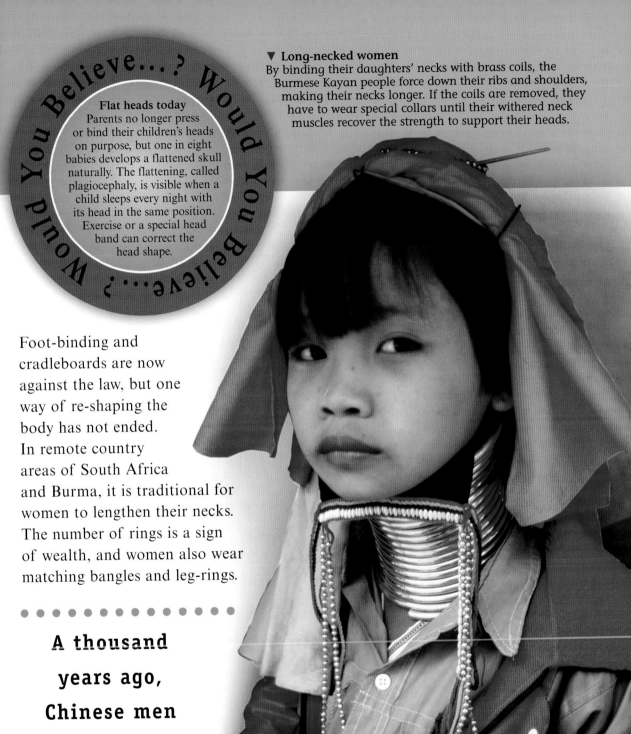

Flat heads today
Parents no longer press or bind their children's heads on purpose, but one in eight babies develops a flattened skull naturally. The flattening, called plagiocephaly, is visible when a child sleeps every night with its head in the same position. Exercise or a special head band can correct the head shape.

▼ **Long-necked women**
By binding their daughters' necks with brass coils, the Burmese Kayan people force down their ribs and shoulders, making their necks longer. If the coils are removed, they have to wear special collars until their withered neck muscles recover the strength to support their heads.

Foot-binding and cradleboards are now against the law, but one way of re-shaping the body has not ended. In remote country areas of South Africa and Burma, it is traditional for women to lengthen their necks. The number of rings is a sign of wealth, and women also wear matching bangles and leg-rings.

A thousand years ago, Chinese men would not marry a woman if her feet had not been bound

Skin Deep

SMOOTH, BLANK AND seamless, human skin is like an artist's canvas. No wonder some of us can't resist decorating it. Skin renews itself regularly, so marks on it soon fade. The only way to make them permanent is by tattooing (injecting dye under the skin) or by cutting to make scars.

Skin art is ancient, but faded from use in Europe as Christianity spread. Some Christians believed that their holy book, the Bible, forbade marking the skin. Tattooing continued in other parts of the world, especially around the Pacific Ocean.

Would You Believe...?

Tattoos and medicine
In many parts of the world, tattooing was a traditional way of protecting against disease. Samoan people believed that tattoos stopped them getting rheumatism. But tattoos do not stop disease, and may even spread it if the needles used to inject the dye are not perfectly clean.

◀ **Maori faces**
Among the native Maori people of New Zealand, a man without tattoos on his face was once thought of as someone of no importance. The elaborate patterns were originally painfully applied with a sharp bone chisel. Dipping the chisel into soot made the swirling marks permanent.

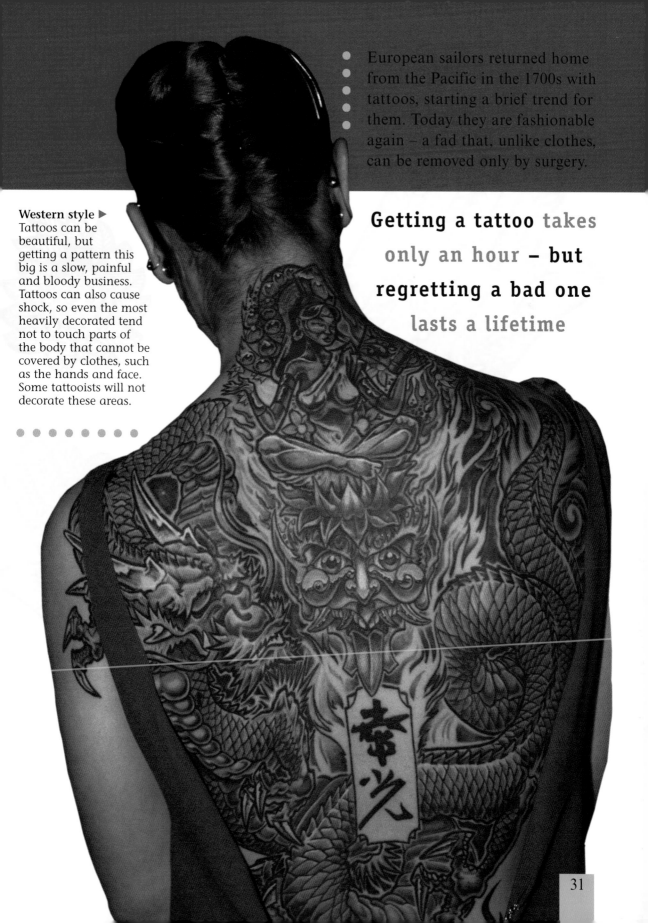

European sailors returned home from the Pacific in the 1700s with tattoos, starting a brief trend for them. Today they are fashionable again – a fad that, unlike clothes, can be removed only by surgery.

Western style ▶
Tattoos can be beautiful, but getting a pattern this big is a slow, painful and bloody business. Tattoos can also cause shock, so even the most heavily decorated tend not to touch parts of the body that cannot be covered by clothes, such as the hands and face. Some tattooists will not decorate these areas.

Getting a tattoo takes only an hour **– but regretting a bad one** lasts a lifetime

31

My Feet are Killing Me

DANCING, WALKING, jogging or just posing, a beautiful shoe shouts, "I've got style!" For centuries, the fashionable have splashed out on their feet, paying cobblers to make colourful and sometimes crazy footwear. At times, the styles have been so extreme that those who wore them couldn't walk.

Poulaines ▶
These shoes from the 15th century got their name, poulaines, from the French word for Poland – where they were first made. As fashions changed, the pointed toes grew longer and longer, until they were twice the length of the feet inside them.

◀ Chopines
Chopines were a type of shoe with a towering sole, fashionable during the 16th and 17th centuries. They were particularly popular in Italy: women in the city of Venice wore chopines 75 cm (2.5 ft) high. This Venetian example is made of silk, wood and leather.

These deliberately useless shoes showed that the owner was rich and never needed to walk more than a few steps. The shoes of poorer people were usually practical, comfortable and watertight because they were always on their feet working.

Would You Believe...? Would You Believe...?

Stomping in stilettos
The pressure underneath a stiletto heel is higher than that under an elephant's foot. Stiletto shoes concentrate all of a woman's weight on to an area no bigger than a fingernail, and the enormous downward force is enough to leave a trail of dents in a polished wooden floor.

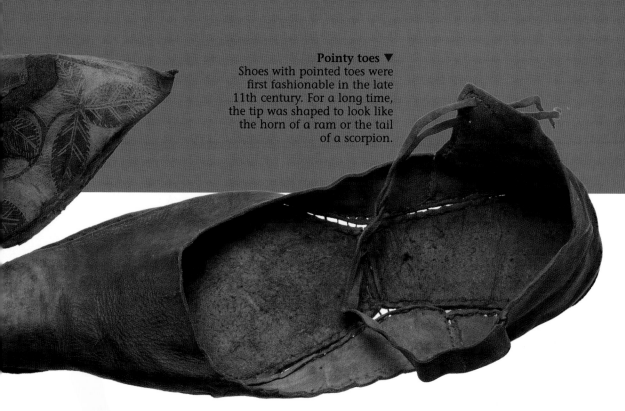

Pointy toes ▼
Shoes with pointed toes were first fashionable in the late 11th century. For a long time, the tip was shaped to look like the horn of a ram or the tail of a scorpion.

High heels were invented in Persia to keep feet out of the burning desert sand

Today, fashions in shoes change quickly, but surprisingly few styles are really new. Platform soles and pointy toes are centuries old. Only the stiletto has a short history – it was invented in Italy in the 1950s.

▲ Pattens
Shoe styles from the past were at their swankiest when the streets were muddiest. The way to keep expensive silk and velvet shoes clean was to slip them into pattens. These extra soles lifted your feet clear of the filth.

Deadly high heels ▲
Tall, narrow and dangerously pointed, stiletto heels were named after the thick-bladed daggers once used by Italian assassins. Though they make the leg look longer, they also make walking difficult and uncomfortable.

33

The Unkindest
Cut of All

T HE FIRST PEOPLE to benefit from modern plastic surgery were not vain men and women, but injured soldiers. Blasted by shells and bombs in World War I (1914–1918), they had their shattered faces reconstructed by patient surgeons and dentists.

Wartime experience gave surgeons new skills. In the USA, a few began to use them to improve angular noses and remove wrinkles with "face lifts". Breast reduction began in the 1920s, but enlargement was not routine until the 1960s.

◀ **The first nose-job**
Plastic surgery started in India some 2,000 years ago with the first nose-jobs. Removal of the nose was a punishment for crimes such as stealing. Surgeons rebuilt it with a leaf-shaped patch of skin cut from the forehead. Flipped and lowered, it grew into a new nose. Wooden breathing tubes kept the nostrils open.

Changing faces ▲
Cosmetic surgeons today can change the appearance of the face – and even make a man look like a woman. British celebrity Pete Burns had a nose-job and collagen (animal protein) injections to model himself a face (main picture) that he believed better fitted his personality.

Obsession with youth and beauty has made cosmetic surgery big business. But many of the operations carried out are unnecessary, and some of the clinics that perform minor treatments use untrained staff. Patients whose operations are botched need costly corrective treatment.

Not the knife

For a few, cosmetic surgery is essential. But for most of us, exercise, less sun and stress and a healthier diet are safer, cheaper ways to improve our appearance.

One 15th-century German surgeon could "make a new nose if it has been lopped off and the dogs have eaten it"

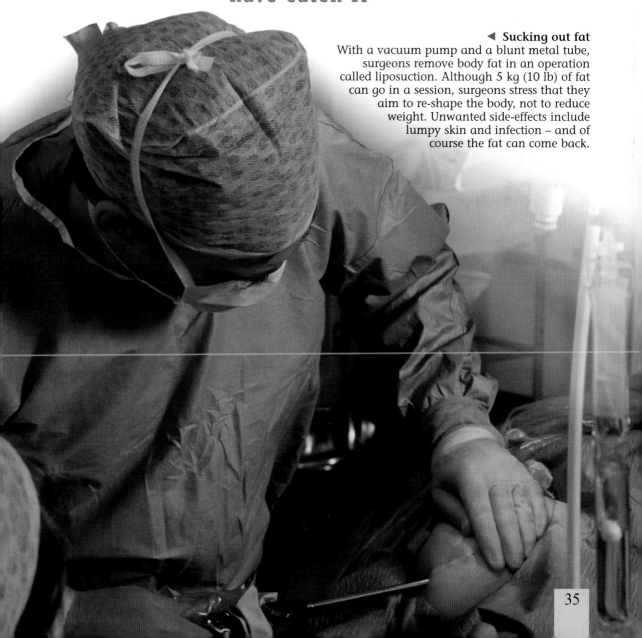

◀ **Sucking out fat**
With a vacuum pump and a blunt metal tube, surgeons remove body fat in an operation called liposuction. Although 5 kg (10 lb) of fat can go in a session, surgeons stress that they aim to re-shape the body, not to reduce weight. Unwanted side-effects include lumpy skin and infection – and of course the fat can come back.

Why Stop
at the Ear?

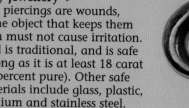

P ROUDLY PIERCED
punks may not know it, but
their punctured lips, noses,
ears, brows and tongues celebrate
a form of body decoration that
is older than history. Nose-rings
are mentioned in the Bible, and
some mummies from ancient
Egypt have pierced ears.

Ear-piercing has always been
popular for women, but in Europe
and the USA few men wore
earrings until the hippie era
of the 1960s. Body piercing began
in the American homosexual
community some ten years later,
and the trend spread.

● ● ● ● ● ● ● ● ● ● ● ● ● ● ● ● ●

◀ **Lip plates**
To make themselves more beautiful, Mursi
women of southwest Ethiopia insert clay
plates into cuts made in their lower lips.
Gradually increasing the size of plate
stretches the piercing to the diameter of a
saucer. Many also stretch their ear-lobes
with plugs in a similar way.

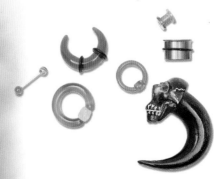

Radical or safe?

The risk of infection from a botched piercing is real, so don't try piercing even an ear-lobe at home. Avoid cheap jewellery and follow hygiene instructions carefully to avoid infection and speed up the healing of the hole.

King of the rings ▶

Cuban Luis Antonio Aguero claims to be the most pierced man in the world. Here, he is wearing 175 pieces of jewellery. Since this picture was taken, he has doubled the number of holes in his head.

Would You Believe...?

Pierced pirates
For a swashbuckling pirate, a gold hoop earring is essential – or is it? Piercing for men was fashionable in the 1500s, but they wore pearls and jewels in their ears, not hoops. And fashion conscious men of the 18th century – pirates included – would never dream of wearing earrings.

The Karankawa Indians of the Texas coast wore small pieces of cane through their pierced nipples

◀ Aztec lip plug
An Aztec nobleman would have worn this plug through his pierced lower lip in about 1500. At about 6 cm (2.5 in) long, this lip plug is as big as some of the most extreme lip ornaments of today. The shaft is made from rock crystal, and the ends are gold.

37

All My Own Teeth

AT FASHIONABLE parties in the past there was little laughter. The jokes were funny enough, but guests kept their lips shut to hide their rotten teeth. Dental care improved in the 20th century, but only the rich could afford it. Just 40 years ago, four out of five older people had no teeth of their own.

The famous and fashionable hid their gaps with dentures (false teeth). Until about 1790, when porcelain dentures became popular, dentists carved them from bone or ivory, or took teeth from animals or from the dead.

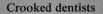

Buying teeth
Wealthy people of the late 18th century found an alternative to dentures. Their dentists pulled out their bad teeth and pushed healthy teeth bought from poor children into the holes. These "live tooth transplants" lasted ten years.

First falsies ▶
In the 7th century BCE, the Etruscan people of Italy filled gaps using extracted teeth. They fixed them to gold bands that slipped over the remaining teeth. Nobody thought of a better way of holding teeth in place for another 2,500 years.

The fashion in 9th century Mayan Mexico was to decorate front teeth with jade and turquoise stones

◀ **Porcelain smile**
French dentist Nicolas Dubois de Chémant was the first to make successful porcelain teeth. This cartoon from 1798 shows a potential patient admiring a porcelain smile.

▼ **Famous teeth**
In 16th century England false teeth were rare, so Queen Elizabeth I packed her mouth with cloth to fill out her sunken face. American president George Washington was not much luckier. His elk and human dentures were held together with powerful springs.

For those needing more than one or two teeth, wars provided a wonderful opportunity. When great battles ended, scavengers with pliers moved among the dead (and nearly dead) pulling teeth to sell. After the 1815 battle of Waterloo, London's rich wore "Waterloo teeth".

▲ **Washington kept his mouth shut to hide his dentures.**

Hippo teeth ▶
Ivory (the tusks of elephants and the teeth of hippopotamuses) supplied the raw materials for countless expensive sets of dentures. The plates and back teeth of this pair are carved from hippo ivory; the front teeth are human.

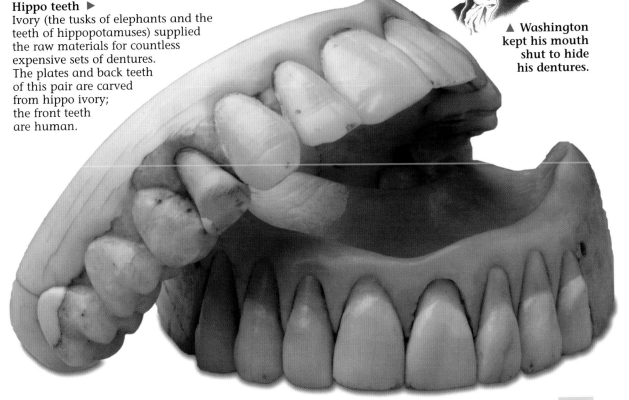

39

Makeup and Beauty

◀ **Greek rouge**
To redden their cheeks, ancient Greek women used the roots of alkanet – a plant of the forget-me-not family. Its red colour contrasted with the white powder used elsewhere on their faces.

PAINTED WITH rouge and eye-liner, a beautiful face gazes at us with confidence. Apart from her hat, this woman could be a catwalk model, but she is from the 12th century BCE. As an Egyptian queen, her makeup would have been prepared by a slave-girl.

Over the following centuries, there has rarely been a time when women, and sometimes men, too, have not coloured their faces for beauty – or to disguise their age.

◀ **Palace chic**
In this portrait sculpture, Queen Nefertiti's eyes are outlined with kohl (see page 42), and her eyebrows are painted. She is not, however, wearing the blue or green eyeshadow that was popular with Egyptian women.

▲ **Egyptian palette**
The ancient Egyptian name for makeup palettes like this one sounded the same as their word for "protect". Copper minerals used in some Egyptian eye makeup helped to prevent eye disease.

From Egyptian eyeliner to lipstick from Ur (now in Iraq), most makeup has ancient origins. Women relied on cosmetics made at home or by hairdressers and pharmacists until they were first mass-produced during the 20th century.

Egyptian workmen went on strike **in 1158** BCE **because they** ran out of eye makeup

Would You Believe...? Would You Believe...?

Lipstick or witchcraft?
Britain's law-makers passed a law against lipstick in 1770. They decided that: "Women found guilty of trapping men into marriage by cosmetics could be tried for witchcraft". In Pennsylvania, USA, men could divorce their wives if they had used makeup when they were dating.

◀ **Beautiful blokes**
In the late 17th century, European men were as painted as their wives. They powdered their faces, then applied rouge and lipstick. Velvet or silk hearts, stars or moons, known as "beauty patches", completed the look.

Cult cosmetics ▶
Makeup doesn't have to make the wearer look younger or more beautiful. Shock-rocker Marilyn Manson uses radical cosmetics to emphasise his already dramatic features. The result is calculated to charm his fans – and terrify their parents.

Poisonous
Potions

MAKEUP TO DIE FOR sounds like a modern advertising slogan but, until laws controlled cosmetic safety, it was the truth. Many kinds of makeup contained poisons that, at best, blistered your skin. At worst, they killed you.

White face powders were among the most dangerous. The main ingredient of ceruse – the powder that every fashionable 14th century lady wore – was poisonous lead. To redden their cheeks, wealthy men and women commonly used vermilion. This fabulously expensive colour contained mercury – another poison.

Would You Believe...?

Murderous makeup
17th century Italian Tofana di Adamo sold a face-whitening makeup called *Aqua tofana* to other women. When 600 husbands died, Tofana was arrested. She confessed that the makeup contained deadly arsenic. Her customers used it to poison their husbands and inherit their money.

▲ Deadly nightshade
The Latin name for the deadly nightshade plant is *belladonna*, meaning "beautiful lady". This name comes from its use – drops of the plant oil make the pupil of the eye bigger and more attractive. The plant's English name reveals its other quality – if swallowed, it kills.

Kohl eyeliner ▶
This 3,300-year-old glass tube from Egypt once held kohl eyeliner, which was made from antimony. Small doses of this metallic element can cause headaches, dizziness and depression. Larger doses are deadly.

16th century women used oil of vitriol (sulphuric acid) as a skin cleanser

Poisons in clothes

Fashionable clothes and shoes have never been as toxic as makeup, but the people who make them have often suffered. Hatters, for instance, died of mercury poisoning, and the lives of leather workers were made shorter by the chemicals they used in tanning (treating animal skins to convert them to leather).

▲ **Pale and interesting**
The white ceruse powder that England's Queen Elizabeth I used to paint her face scarred her skin. To hide the marks, she applied ever-thicker layers. By the time she died, Elizabeth's face looked like a white mask.

Most cosmetics today are safe, but there are still dangerous levels of mercury in some skin-lightening products. And a few labels hide dirty secrets: certain expensive anti-ageing creams are made from the tissue of pregnant women.

Mad as a hatter ▶
The Mad Hatter in Lewis Carroll's *Alice's Adventures in Wonderland* was driven mad by his job. Hatters used mercury to roughen the fibres of felt hats. It slowly poisoned them, causing twitching limbs, confused speech, mental illness and death.

What's so Weird about That?

OUTRAGEOUS, DARING, extravagant – and sometimes even dangerous – fashion makes our world brighter and our lives livelier. Although we gasp at daring catwalk styles, a glance through this book shows that, in a different time or place, someone has almost always dressed in an even more amazing way.

These styles from different cultures and ages make fashion more interesting and varied. You may not want to wear a towering wig, but the world would be a duller place if nobody ever had.

◀ **The catwalk**
Catwalk models show off styles that only the very wealthiest can buy. Through *haute couture* (high fashion) like this, a few top designers control the clothes millions of us wear – whether we like it or not.

Fashion slaves
Fashion may seem like fun but, as you've seen, it can be ridiculous and harmful, too. Looking just the same as everyone else may be reassuring, but it is also expensive and wasteful. Why should this summer's colours, fabrics and styles be different from last summer's?

Don't be afraid to escape from the herd: be yourself, and wear something completely different

44

Find out More

You can learn more about costume and fashion by checking out these websites and places to visit.

Websites

Costume drama game
http://www.museumofcostume.co.uk/htmlContent/game.htm
Test your knowledge of fashion from four eras.

Design a textile
http://www.vam.ac.uk/vastatic/microsites/british_galleries/designa/textile/textile.html
Mix and match colours and patterns, then print out your fabric sample.

Fashion era
http://www.fashion-era.com
The place to look for hard facts about fashion.

Kimonos
http://web-japan.org/kidsweb/virtual/kimono/top.html
Find out about traditional Japanese costume, and create your own kimono.

Corsets
http://www.vam.ac.uk/collections/fashion/corset/index.html
Discover the secret history of corsets and crinolines with this Victoria & Albert Museum virtual exhibit.

Henna tattoos
http://www.mehendiworld.com
The story of *mehendi* (henna tattoos), with practical instructions and designs to copy.

All about shoes
http://www.allaboutshoes.ca/en
Learn about high heels and more on this website.

History of sneakers
http://www.sneakerhead.com/sneaker-history-p1.html
All you need to know about sneakers and trainers.

Places to visit

The Victoria & Albert Museum
Cromwell Road
London SW7 2RL
Telephone: 020 7942 2000
Website: http://www.vam.ac.uk/collections/index.html
This vast museum in London is a treasure trove for fashion fans, with beautifully displayed original costumes from the past, and constantly changing special exhibitions. The V&A is not just fashion: its collection includes examples from many other kinds of art, design and craft.

Bath Museum of Costume
Bennett Street
Bath BA1 2QH
Telephone: 01225 477 173
Website: http://www.museumofcostume.co.uk
Displays at this museum in the centre of Bath illustrate changing styles of dress over the last 400 years. There are regular themed shows, and the permanent exhibition is divided into three sections: fashion before 1800; 19th century clothes; and costume since 1900.

Shambellie House Museum of Costume
New Abbey
Dumfriesshire DG2 8HQ
Telephone: 01387 850 375
Website: http://www.nms.ac.uk/costume/home/index.asp
In this Victorian house near Dumfries, the main rooms are shown as if frozen in time, displaying costumes from seven periods between 1882 and 1952.

Manchester Gallery of Costume
Platt Hall
Rusholme
Manchester M14 5LL
Telephone: 0161 224 5217
Website: http://www.manchestergalleries.org/html/costume/goc_home.jsp
One of the largest collections of costumes and accessories in Britain. Unusually, the gallery shows not only high fashion, but also the clothes of ordinary working people.

Third-party website addresses referred to in this publication are provided by Oxford University Press in good faith and for information only. Oxford University Press disclaims any responsibility for the material contained therein.

Glossary

Did you read anything you didn't understand? Some of the more complicated and unusual terms used in this book are explained here.

armour
Protective clothing worn in battle to prevent injuries.

arsenic
Poisonous metal-like chemical: one-twentieth of a teaspoonful would kill an adult.

boycott
Way of protesting by not buying or using a product or service.

catwalk
Long, raised stage along which models walk in fashion shows.

cobbler
Worker who makes or repairs shoes.

dandy
Elegantly dressed man who takes great care about his appearance.

denture
Artificial teeth, and the plate or frame that holds them in place.

embroidery
Decorative, colourful pattern of stitches on a garment.

extinction
Killing or death of the world's very last plant or animal of a particular kind.

flapper
Woman from the 1920s who did not obey traditional rules of dress and behaviour.

geisha
Traditional female Japanese performer, and paid entertainer of men.

knight
Armoured warrior of the 12th–16th centuries.

Maori
Native people of New Zealand.

mercury
Poisonous, shiny, silver-coloured liquid metal.

Mohican
Hairstyle in which the scalp is shaved, apart from a narrow central strip.

pharmacist
Worker who makes or supplies healing drugs.

plastic surgery
Surgery to change the body or face, either to correct deformed or damaged features (reconstructive surgery), or to make the patient look prettier (cosmetic surgery).

porcelain
Fragile, glassy type of fine-quality pottery.

punk
Freedom movement that began in the 1970s, with its own distinctive, outrageous styles of dress, dance and music.

revolution
When many people rise up to take power away from an unpopular government.

silk
Fine, smooth fabric made from threads spun by a moth.

stiletto
Long, slim knife, and the high shoe heel named after it.

surgeon
Doctor trained in surgery (cutting open the human body).

tailor
Worker who makes or adjusts clothes.

tanning
Treatment of animal skins to make them into soft, bendy leather.

tattoo
Permanent pattern on the skin, made by rubbing or injecting colouring materials into tiny pricks or cuts.

tiara
Small, jewelled, woman's crown, now usually worn only by queens or brides.

uniform
Matching clothing worn to show authority or membership of a group, especially military or official groups such as armies and police forces.

witchcraft
The practice of secret, magic actions, usually aiming to change or foresee future events.

Index

Picture credits

The publisher would like to thank the following for their kind permission to reproduce their photographs:

Position key: c=centre; b=bottom; l=left; r=right; t=top

Cover: Front: tr: Dynamic Graphics Group/Creatas/Alamy; cr: Getty Images/Chip Simons; bl: Mary Evans Picture Library/Alamy; tl: Getty Images/Kenny Johnson. Background: OUP/Photodisc.

4c: R Sheridan/Ancient Art & Architecture Collection Ltd; 5l: Sunset Boulevard/Corbis; 5r: Doug Peters/allactiondigital/Empics; 6r: Brooklyn Museum of Art/Corbis; 7l: Gianni Dagli Orti/Corbis; 8l: Araldo de Luca/Corbis; 9bc: Museum of London/Heritage Image Partnership; 10r: Museum of London/Heritage Image Partnership; 10bl: Darren Sawyer; 11b: Historical Picture Archive/Corbis; 11tl: Akg-Images/Erich Lessing; 11l: Akg-Images/Erich Lessing; 11cl: Akg-Images/Erich Lessing; 12r: Araldo de Luca/Corbis; 13b: Hulton-Deutsch Collection/Corbis; 14l: Mary Evans Picture Library; 15r: 20th Century Fox/The Kobal Collection; 16br: Michael Malsan Historic Photographs/Corbis; 16l: Museum of London/Heritage Image Partnership; 17r: Adrianna Williams/ Zefa/Corbis; 19bl: Museum of London/Heritage Image Partnership; 19r: Tim Graham/Corbis; 20r: Conde Nast Archive/Corbis; 21r: Darren Sawyer; 21c: Roderick Eime-Monolith; 22l: Mary Evans Picture Library; 23r: Matthew Mendelsohn; 23cl: Darren Sawyer; 24r: Museum of London/Heritage Image Partnership; 25tl: Hulton-Deutsch Collection/Corbis; 26l: Museum of London/Heritage Image Partnership; 27t: Museum of London/Heritage Image Partnership; 27br: Akg-Images; 28bc: Science Museum/Science and Society Picture Library; 28cr: Lake County Museum/Corbis; 29r: Daniel Laine/Corbis; 30cr: Wellcome Trust; 31c: Gene Blevins/Corbis; 32cl: V&A; 32t: Museum of London/Heritage Image Partnership; 33bl: V&A; 33br: Saunders Photographic; 34bl: Wellcome Trust; 34c: Steve Jennings/Corbis; 34r: Rune Hellestad/Corbis; 35c: Science Photo Library; 36l: Photo Researchers/Corbis; 36b: Akg-Images/Erich Lessing; 37tr: Hussein Akhtar/Corbis Sygma; 37b: Akg-Images/Erich Lessing; 38r: Science Museum/Science and Society Picture Library; 39t: Science Museum/Science and Society Picture Library; 39b: Science Museum/Science and Society Picture Library; 40cr: DK Limited/Corbis; 40l: Archivo Iconografico, S.A./Corbis; 41br: Hubert Boesl/dpa/Corbis; 42r: The British Museum/Heritage Image Partnership; 43tl: Ann Ronan Picture Library/Heritage Image Partnership; 43br: Lake County Museum/Corbis; 44bl: Stephane Cardinale/People